Pentagon Papers

Edited by J-Powers

P PowerPlayz Publishing

PowerPlayz Publishing
PowerPlayz.com -- Los Angeles

Pentagon Papers

Recently abridged edition for the Millennial Generation
Copyright © 2012 J-Powers

First Printing, 2012
Printed in the United States of America
ISBN 978-0-9859175-0-0

Library of Congress Control Number: 2012912814

For the next generation

Contents

Acknowledgements

Pentagon Papers began as a stage work in 2011. I am grateful to the many people and organizations that have helped me bring this vital information into currency for a new generation.

To the people of Torrance, California, and their elected officials for supporting the theater series Works in Progress in which this endeavor was first developed to commemorate the 40th anniversary of the publication of the Pentagon Papers.

To the actors who participated in bringing that developmental project to life: Tom Brewer, Mike Campbell, John Crowther, Perry Daniel, Pat Furey, Michael Grenie, Jenny Kang, Emily Kuroda, Diana Mann, Joseph Murray, Paul Nowatka, VyVy Nguyen, Frank Pepito, Joel Polis, Ken Seeraty, Perry Shields, Bill Sutherland, Ann Song, John Wong, Jani Wang, Bill Wolski, and Michael Yama.

To Vietnam Veterans of America for its association with this project at that early stage, in particular the members of Chapter 53.

To the cast, crew, and theater staff of Santa Monica Playhouse for the 2012 production from which the text of this publication is derived: Robert Adams, Jeffrey Ashkin, Chris DeCarlo, Caroline Do, Serena Dolinsky, Mark Jacobson, Stephen Juhl, Dave Kirkpatrick, Paul Linke, JR Mangels, Diana Mann, Amanda Martindale, Cricket S. Myers, Evelyn Rudie, Brian Sounalath, George Vennes III, and Sandra Zeitzew.

To the Center for Cultural Innovation for support of that 2012 production through its Artists' Resource Completion grant.

To USA Projects for its assistance in fund development for this publication that serves as a completion project to that production.

To Pat Acosta, Barbara Barker, Ruth Brugger, Anna Gee, Eileen Haussmann, Elsie Inase, Bernice Joffe, Gretchen Kanne, Richard Lerner, Cheryl Lyons,

Christine Mei, Claudia Mullin, Sheri Lee Myers, James Powers, Carole Ross, John Spokes, and Moe Stavnezer for funding support of this publication.

To Paul Glickler for editing assistance and valuable suggestions.

To Daniel Ellsberg and Anthony Russo for bringing this information into the light of day.

To my wife DeBorah Green for enduring love and support.

On the Web

To view a video, the first of four parts, documenting a performance of this material, scan this code or go to: https://vimeo.com/52488981

Foreword

The Pentagon Papers is one of the greatest works of American letters. It is great because of its sheer size and the manner in which it was created. When it was completed, the Papers totaled about 7,000 pages. Three-dozen analysts worked on the text, each of them writing their separate volumes in the same conference room in the Pentagon. It was completed in less than one year.

The Papers is particularly great because it provides insight to the inner workings of the highest levels of American power during the course of 23 years. A cast of characters is ever-changing, but the processes, decisions, and deceits remain the same. The document reveals how that power actually operates.

If you are someone who came of age after the Carter Administration (1977-81), it is unlikely that you know about the Pentagon Papers except as it has been referenced during massive WikiLeaks disclosures. This recently abridged edition has been conceived specifically so that you can experience the broad scope of that entire original work in one or two sittings. In addition, there are online resources included to expand your experience. Use your QR (quick response) reader or Web browser to access these resources.

The aim of this publication, drawn exclusively from the original work, is to restore the currency of the Papers to a new generation who find their nation engaged in another "endless war." This new generation will discover that we have been here before and that it will not end without concerted effort to impose transparency and accountability on our leaders.

J-Powers
Los Angeles

Note: throughout the publication, all text between brackets "[ ]" has been written by the editor to facilitate easier reading and greater comprehension.

Introduction

The Pentagon Papers, or the Vietnam Study as it was know among a very small circle of people within the U.S. Defense Department, was a reconstruction in narrative form of the step-by-step decisions that brought America to have a half-million military personnel in that Southeast Asian nation during the mid-1960s. The history of this decision making began in the aftermath of World War II and extended to 1968. America's role in the conflict continued, however, until 1975.

The study was commissioned by Secretary of Defense Robert McNamara in 1967, as he was having grave doubts about America's ability to succeed militarily in Vietnam. While classified, the project was given a relatively low-level security clearance: "top secret-sensitive." McNamara did not want his boss, President Lyndon Johnson (1963-68), to know that this study being written; he was certain that the President would put a stop to it. McNamara initiated this project because he wanted to leave a record of how the U.S. got into the predicament of a seemingly endless war. His aim may have been to prevent such an experience in the future.

One of the few people who read the study in its entirety was Daniel Ellsberg, a defense analyst who wrote about the early years of President John Kennedy's administration (1961-63) for the Study. By his own account, Ellsberg was undergoing a personal transformation with regard to the Vietnam War. He was growing increasingly skeptical. As any person working in the upper echelons of government, he was aware that lying was a commonplace occurrence when dealing with the press, the public, and other government officials. Reading the entire work and searching for patterns while later employed at the RAND Corporation, a defense think-tank located in Santa Monica, California, he realized that the level of deceit and betrayal was extraordinary and profoundly self-defeating. Furthermore, the lying was about to increase.

Ellsberg knew—as did only a few others at the time—that President Richard Nixon (1969-74), despite his campaign slogan to achieve "peace with honor," was about to carry on the bombing strategy at a massively increased level. This policy of devastation would be conducted in secrecy.

Ellsberg made the decision in 1970 to put his liberty at risk by making copies of the Vietnam Study and circulating them to elected officials. He tried to raise the alarm that the war was not going away. Ellsberg also provided access to the Study for the New York Times, which published some of the information in 1971. It was during the course of the subsequent courtroom battle for the right to publish that the Study became commonly known as the Pentagon Papers.

Bringing this history of deception and betrayal into light did not have the effect that Ellsberg sought. It made people very skeptical of the government, but it did not end the war—at least not immediately.

Among President Nixon's responses to the publication of the Pentagon Papers—which he gleefully recognized tarnished the image of his nemesis President Kennedy—was the decision to create a White House team of "plumbers," operatives whose mission was to find and to leak additional damaging information about "enemies" to the media. Members of this team were arrested for burglary of the Democratic National Committee in the Watergate complex one year later. In his subsequent attempt to defeat his impeachment in the Senate, Nixon applied the last of his waning influence on a vote in favor of himself rather than to uphold his pledge to the Saigon government and urge a resumption of the bombing campaign against the compelling forces of the Viet Cong and the North Vietnamese Army.

1

Independence

With the end of World War II, Vietnamese nationalists fight to stop France from reasserting colonial control

Significant misunderstanding has developed concerning U.S. policy towards Indochina in the decade of World War II. A number of historians have held that anti-colonialism governed U.S. policy up until 1950, when containment of communism supervened. Other commentators have described U.S. policy as consistently condoning the re-imposition of French colonial power in Indochina, with a disregard for the nationalist aspirations of the Vietnamese. Neither interpretation squares with the record. Ambivalence characterized U.S. policy during World War II, and was the root of much subsequent misunderstanding. On the one hand, the U.S. repeatedly reassured the French that its colonial possessions would be returned to it after the war. On the other hand, the U.S. broadly committed itself to support national self-determination, and President Franklin Roosevelt vehemently advocated independence for Indochina.

Roosevelt: France has had the country and its inhabitants for nearly one hundred years, and the people are worse off than they were at the beginning. They are entitled to something better than that.

In November, 1942, [the] Secretary [of State Cordell Hull] submitted to [President Roosevelt] a proposed draft U.S.-U.K. declaration entitled "The Atlantic Charter and National Independence." [The Secretary soon reported that the British] did not like our draft very much. Particularly the word "independence." [Our] inability to work out a common policy with the [British] precluded meaningful discussion on the colonial issue. And with Roosevelt's death in April, 1945, U.S. policy toward the colonial possessions of its allies, and toward Indochina in particular, was in disarray.

Following President [Harry] Truman's entry into office, the U.S. assured

France that it had never questioned French sovereignty over Indochina. Ultimately, U.S. policy was governed neither by the principles of the Atlantic Charter, nor by [Roosevelt's] anticolonialism but by the dictates of military strategy and by British intransigence. The United States, concentrating its forces against Japan, accepted British military primacy in Southeast Asia. In August, 1945, [the Viet Minh,] Vietnamese resistance forces [to the Japanese] under Ho Chi Minh, seized power in [the major northern city] Hanoi and shortly thereafter demanded the abdication of the Japanese puppet, Emperor Bao Dai. On V-J Day, Ho Chi Minh had proclaimed in Hanoi the establishment of the Democratic Republic of Vietnam. The DRV ruled as the only civil government in all of Vietnam for a period of about twenty days. On September 23, with the knowledge of the British Commander [in the major southern city] Saigon, French forces overthrew the local DRV government and declared French authority restored.

2

War Begins

**Vietnamese nationalists struggle to find a
compromise with France, but are betrayed**

The fighting between the French and
the Vietnamese, which began with the
French coup d'etat, spread from Saigon
[and extended throughout the country.]
The French were about to send an in-
vading force into [the major northern
port] Haiphong, when Ho stuck a peace
accord. Vietnam was to be recognized
as a free state with France pledging to
ratify the decision pending a popular
referendum. [While French leaders went
back and forth on this accord,] Ho made
repeated overtures to the United States,
Britain, the United Nations, China, and
the USSR. His letters presented elo-
quent appeals for U.S. intervention in
Vietnam on the grounds of the principles embodied in the Atlantic Charter
and the UN Charter. The U.S. appears
to have adhered to a policy of looking to
the French rather than to [the] Nationalists for constructive steps toward Viet-

namese independence. In Hanoi, on December 19, 1946, Vietnamese troops, after several days of mounting animosity, cut off the city's water and electricity and attacked French posts using small arms, mortar, and artillery. The fighting flared across the north, and two days later the guerrilla war in the south quickened pace. The French responded to the initial attacks with a savagery which rendered increasingly remote restoration of status quo ante.

The French Premier spoke repeatedly in the spring of 1947 of an imminent end to the "military phase" of the crisis, and of the beginning of a "constructive phase." But in what was to become a pattern of expectation and frustration, [France] discovered that its military forces were incapable of controlling even the principal lines of communication in Vietnam. By the summer, the French Government was aware that the situation was at an impasse. It was with [the former Japanese puppet Emperor] Bao Dai, not Ho Chi Minh, that the French elected to negotiate for a political settlement. French emissaries approached Bao Dai with terms not unlike those Ho

Chi Minh had negotiated earlier: unity and independence within the French Union. [But despite settlement with the former puppet, the fight with the Viet Minh continued.]

On the web
To learn more about Ho Chi Minh, scan this code or go to: http://en.wikipedia.org/wiki/Ho_Chi_Minh

3

U.S. Gets Involved

As the U.S. moves to contain Communism globally, France rebrands its colonial ambitions to secure American aid

The first suggestion that the U.S. became tangibly involved in Vietnam appears in a conversation of the U.S. Ambassador [Jefferson Caffery] with the French Foreign Office in September, 1948.

Caffery: I informed the minister that [the] U.S. was willing to consider assisting [his] government with respect to [the] matter of financial aid for Indochina but could not give consideration to altering [our] present policy unless real progress [is] made in reaching [a] non-Communist solution.

Events in China, [the victory of Mao Zedong's forces,] brought the United States to a new awareness of the vigor of communism in Asia and to a sense of urgency over its containment. [In June, 1949,] the staff of the National Security

Council [began] reexamining U.S. policy toward Asia.

NSC: The extension of communist authority in China represents a grievous political defeat. If southeast Asia also is swept by communism, we shall have suffered a major political rout the repercussions of which will be felt throughout the rest of the world.

In the closing months of 1949, the course of U.S. policy was set to block further communist expansion in Asia. On December 30, the French signed implementing agreements relating to the transfer of internal administration to Bao Dai's State of Vietnam. [Soon after,] President Truman approved U.S. recognition for Bao Dai, [which] was followed swiftly by French requests for U.S. aid. The United States thereafter was directly involved in the developing tragedy in Vietnam.

4

"Go Along"

U.S. support for the war grows, but so does its frustration with the French effort

U.S. assistance, which began modestly with $10 million in 1950, reached [$1 billion] in 1954, at which time it accounted for 78% of the cost of the French war burden. The United States attempted to use its military assistance to gain leverage over French policies, but was severely constrained in what it could do. Allocation of U.S. aid to [Vietnam] had to be made solely through the French. Thus, [the U.S.] was not allowed to control the dispensing of supplies. [U.S.] officers were not given the necessary freedom to develop intelligence information. [And] information supplied by the French was limited, and often unreliable or deliberately misleading. [Still,] the most fundamental fact was that the French were carrying on a war which the United States considered to be essential. [The U.S. itself was engaged in a land war in Korea.]

Thus, the French were always able to threaten simply to end the war by pulling out. The temptation [was] to "go along" with the French until the Viet Minh was defeated.

[Several] events in 1953 served to deepen the American commitment. The first was the arrival of a Republican Administration following a long period in which the G.O.P. had persistently accused the Truman Administration of being responsible for the "loss" of China to communism. In addition, the Viet Minh invasion of Laos in the spring and the deepening war weariness in France served to strengthen those who favored a more assertive policy in Indochina. The question to be faced was: how far was the U.S. prepared to go in terms of force commitments to ensure that Indochina stayed out of Communist hands? The Defense Department pressed for an early determination of the forces the U.S. would be willing to dispatch in an emergency situation. The Chief of Naval Operations proposed that the U.S. decide immediately to employ combat forces on the "reasonable assurance of strong indigenous support of our forces," whether or not the French Government approved. But the Director of the Office of Foreign Military Affairs [Adm. Arthur Davis observed:]

Davis: Involvement of U.S. forces in the Indochina war should be avoided at all practical costs. If National Policy determines no other alternative, the U.S. should not be self-duped into believing the possibility of partial involvement-- such as "Naval and Air units only." One cannot go over Niagara Falls in a barrel only slightly.

5

Dien Bien Phu

French forces suffer a spectacular defeat, and the tables turn on U.S. efforts to contain Communism

[The "emergency situation" came sooner than expected. In March 1954,] the Viet Minh began its assault upon Dien Bien Phu. This fortress in northern Vietnam was to take on a political and psychological importance far out of proportion to its actual strategic value because of the upcoming Geneva Conference, [an international gathering convened to discuss primarily a settlement of the Korean War, but to which a political settlement of the French-Viet Minh war had been added]. The Viet Minh foresaw that a show of decisive force would markedly strengthen their hand at the conference. The Viet Minh were greatly helped by a substantial increase in the level of Chinese military aid including artillery and radar.

As the battle developed, the optimism which had pervaded Washington statements on the war was replaced with the conviction that unless new steps were taken, the French were bound to go under. Accordingly, [U.S. Secretary of State John Foster] Dulles in his discussions with [the French] went beyond the question of immediate assistance to the garrison at Dien Bien Phu and broached the possible establishment of a regional defense arrangement for Southeast Asia.

Dulles: If the Communist forces were to win uncontested control over Indochina or any substantial part thereof, they would surely resume the same pattern of aggression against the other free peoples in that area. The Philippines, Australia and New Zealand...the entire western Pacific area would be strategically endangered.

[Dulles] then went on call for "united action." The French response to [his] proposal was overtaken by military events at Dien Bien Phu. The [French] Foreign Minister contended on April 5 that the fate of [the garrison] would be decided in the next ten days. The United States was now being called upon to act quickly and unilaterally to save a local situation, rather than, as Dulles desired, in concert with Asian and Western Allies. In anticipation of the French request for intervention, Eisenhower decided to consult with Congressional leaders. Secretary Dulles and the [Chairman of the Joint Chiefs of Staff] met with eight Congressmen at the State Department. The Chairman apparently outlined a plan for an air strike on the Viet Minh at Dien Bien Phu using 200 planes from the aircraft carriers Essex and Boxer. An unsuccessful air strike might need to be followed by a second air strike, but ground forces were not envisaged at this stage. The Congressional leaders raised questions about the amount of allied support, about the position of the other Joint Chiefs, about the need for ground forces if a second air strike also failed, and about the danger of a mammoth Chinese intervention which could transform Indochina into another Korean-type war. The Chairman apparently was forced to admit that he was the only one of the Joint Chiefs who favored the intervention plan. [And] Dulles conceded that the allies had not as yet been consulted. In consequence, Dulles, who had been thinking of a joint Congressional resolution authorizing Presidential use of U.S. air-naval power, which it is alleged he had ready in his pocket, left the meeting without the vital support he needed.

The feasibility of American intervention at Dien Bien Phu was finally removed with the fall of that fortress on May 7. The fall of [the garrison], and the failure to organize an intervention through "united action" prior to the opening of the Geneva Conference, led to a reappraisal of the "domino theory" which had been at the center of U.S. policy in Southeast Asia since the late 1940's. Accordingly, four days after the French surrender, Dulles observed:

Dulles: Southeast Asia could be secured even without perhaps Vietnam, Laos, and Cambodia.

6

Geneva

The Viet Minh proposes a shocking settlement, and France accepts to the dismay of its allies

Nine delegations seated at a roundtable to exchange views obscured the fact that true bargaining was not taking place. Proposals were, of course, tabled and debated; but actual give-and-take was reserved for private discussions. Political and ideological differences were so intense, particularly between the American and Chinese representatives, that diplomacy had to be conducted circuitously, with [others] frequently acting as mediators and messengers for delegates unwilling to be found together. In a background briefing for newsmen at Geneva, Dulles gave indication that the United States would dissociate itself from any settlement rather than be party to unacceptable terms.

The first test of U.S. policy came when the French informed Washington of the proposals they intended to make in the opening round. The proposals included a separation of the "civil war" in Vietnam from the Communist aggressions in Cambodia and Laos; a cease-fire, supervised by a well-staffed international authority and followed by political discussions leading to free elections; the regrouping of regular forces of the belligerents into defined zones upon signature of a cease-fire agreement; the disarming of all irregular forces; and a guarantee of the agreements by "the States participating in the Geneva Conference."

[Negative] American perspectives on the likely pattern of the Geneva negotiations were confirmed when the Viet Minh forwarded their first proposal "package." Pham Van Dong, then the Viet Minh's vice-minister for foreign affairs and already a seasoned negotiator with the French, introduced his case with the argument that the Viet Minh were the "stronger" force in "more than three-fourths of the country." He went on to describe the successful administration of this territory by his government, which he said "represents the will of the entire Vietnamese nation." The opposition, the Bao Dai regime, [he] character-ized as "the government of the tempo-rarily occupied zone," [which] did not enjoy popular support and was merely the tool of the French. The meaning of Dong's proposal was clear. A political settlement would precede a military agreement to a cease-fire rather than the reverse.

The question how best to disentangle the opposing armies was most acute and might have brought the conference to a standstill had not Pham Van Dong suddenly reversed his [earlier] position and proposed what amounted to the partitioning of [Vietnam.] What had prompted Dong to introduce [this] ar-rangement may have [been] Sino-Soviet pressure to produce an alternative to proposals that were consistently being rejected by the West. Whatever lay be-hind Dong's gambit, the French were put in the position of being challenged on their prior commitments to the Viet-namese [government of Bao Dai, which had] urged Paris to neither seek nor ac-cept a division of Vietnam. On June 26, Paris formally notified Washington and London that [it] would soon begin direct talks with Pham Van Dong.

Between July 18 and 21, the conferees were able to iron out their differences sufficiently to produce agreements now commonly referred to as the Geneva "accords." The accords consist of military agreements for Vietnam, Cambodia, and Laos to fulfill the conference's primary task of restoring peace to Indochina, and a Final Declaration designed to establish the conditions for future political settlements. The Geneva accords temporarily established two zones of Vietnam separated by a line running roughly along the 17th parallel and further divided by a demilitarized zone. The United States [refused to] formally sign the Geneva accords. [Further,] the U.S. began revising policy toward Indochina as the Conference closed [with an] urgency dictated by the belief that Geneva had been a disaster for the free world.

American qualifications to the accords paled beside those made by [Bao Dai's delegates who] refused to accept a divided country and believed that the

French had brazenly and illegally sold out [their] interests. While it may have been absurd for them to believe that partition was avoidable given Viet Minh strength, their rationale for keeping the country united was, as matters developed, eminently clear-sighted. Partition would be merely a temporary interlude before the renewal of fighting.

On the Web
To learn more about Emperor Bao Dai, scan this code or go to http://en.wikipedia.org/wiki/Bao_Dai

7

Diem

The American formula for government in free Vietnam [in the South] rested on three legs. Independence was first and most important. France must treat Vietnam as an independent sovereign nation, and the U.S. would deal with it on that basis. Secondly, the U.S. would urge Ngo Dinh Diem [a strident anti-communist named as prime minister] to establish a government of national union representative of dominant elements on the political scene. After bringing some stability to the nation, a Constituent Assembly would be called and a constitution drafted to herald the legal dethroning of Emperor Bao Dai and inauguration of democracy. Finally, the formula demanded firm French and U.S. support for Diem. Despite his rigidity, his penchant for a one-man show, and his inability to communicate or deal with people, Diem was a nationalist untainted by past association with either Viet Minh or French. This quality would result in a strong anti-communist South Vietnam. Or so the U.S. thought.

[Before any formula could commence, the new government in the southern zone of Vietnam had to deal with the sects.] The Cao Dai and Hoa Hao sects, basically religious groups with important political interests as well as private French-subsidized armies, [conspired] to overthrow Diem in a coup]. Then, spurred by the knowledge that [such] action would jeopardize American aid, the sects agreed to work with Diem. The Binh Xuyen, [an organization of gangsters and river pirates who controlled the Cholon area of Saigon, had also] considered joining the coalition [government] but pulled out when Diem refused to name their [gang's] leader [as] Minister of the Interior.

The sects had been quiescent but not quiet since [their] ministers had joined the cabinet. The end of French subsidies for [their] armies, however, shook them out of complacency. Sect leaders had wanted to preserve their military forces by integrating, intact, as many units as possible into the National Army. Secondly, the sects wanted substantial government assistance for soldiers forced to leave the military. Most important, they wanted recognition of their areas of influence and Diem's assurance that he would not encroach on their territories. Diem would countenance no part of this.

In February 1955, sect leaders [conspired] with [the gangsters to] put down hostilities among themselves and joined in a United Front of Nationalist Forces. The United Front demanded Diem form a government of large national union. Diem called the Front program an ultimatum. Before dawn on March 28, a paratrooper company loyal to Diem attacked and overcame the gangster-controlled central police headquarters. [The following night,] the [gangsters] struck back. [Their] mortar shells fell on the palace grounds, and [their] troops tried to regain the prefecture. They were repulsed by National

Army troops. The Army then moved to attack the [police headquarters] itself in retaliation, but French officers apparently cut off their supplies to keep [them] on the defensive. The U.S. advised Diem to be patient, that the French were really being helpful by negotiating with the [gangsters]...Sizable sums [of money] were being offered to Army officers and to sect leaders who were remaining loyal to Diem and to entice them into being at least neutral. [A truce was struck.]

After a full day of "soul-searching," the French military chief had been forced to conclude Diem had to go to preserve Vietnam for the free world. The American military chief had been nearing a similar conclusion. [He] left Saigon for [face-to-face] consultations in Washington. Secretary of State] Dulles agreed to consider shifting support to [another leader,] and a message to this effect was sent to Saigon. [Meanwhile], the truce exploded. On April 28, Diem's secretary called [a U.S. counterinsurgency advisor]. He said the palace was under heavy mortar fire, that the President was on another line talking to [the French military chief, who] stated that he couldn't hear any explosions, and the President was holding the mouthpiece out towards the explosions so [he] could hear them. The secretary started to ask [U.S. advisor] what should be done, interrupted himself to say that the President had just ordered the Army to start returning the fire, and hung up. Within nine hours after Diem's order to take the offensive, the Army had driven the [gangsters] back into Cholon. Washington responded with alacrity to Diem's success, superficial though it was. Saigon was told to forget Dulles' earlier message about U.S. willingness to see a change in government.

On the Web
To view a video on Ngo Dinh Diem, scan this code or go to http://www.youtube.com/watch?v=WYMsA2WfZ9M&feature=related

8

No Elections

Although political concessions made to the United States had almost eliminated French presence and influence in Vietnam, France still was obligated to carry out the provisions of the Geneva Accords. The French urgently sought to persuade Diem to accept consultations about the elections scheduled to begin in July 1955. Diem could not bring himself to sit down with the Viet Minh. Consultations would give the appearance of having accepted the Geneva settlement. But another reason was Diem's belief that he could not represent a sovereign nation--or be free of Viet Minh propaganda charges of being a colonialist puppet--until the French were gone. In December, Diem suddenly terminated the accords worked out at the conference and laid down these conditions on which he would consider renewed relations with France.

France had to denounce the Geneva Agreements, to renounce the general elections, to approve openly and without reservation [his] policy to break all relations with the Viet Minh, and of course to call home the [French forces].

There was little France could do. Diem spoke for a government no longer dependent on French support. Eight months later, he finally relaxed his uncompromising stand, but France was never able to meet [its] Geneva obligations concerning the elections, for Diem matched his refusal to consult with the Viet Minh about elections with an adamant refusal to ever hold them. The U.S. did not--as is often alleged--connive with Diem to ignore the elections. U.S. State Department records indicate that Diem's refusal to be bound by the Accords and his opposition to pre-election consultations were at his own initiative. However, the U.S., which had expected elections to be held, and up until May 1955 had fully supported them, shifted its position in the face of Diem's opposition.

The DRV [in the North] repeatedly tried to engage the Geneva machinery, forwarding messages to the Government of South Vietnam, proposing consultations to negotiate "free general elections by secret ballot," and to liberalize north-south relations in general. Each time, the [South] replied with disdain or with silence. The 17th parallel, with its de-militarized zone on either side, became de facto an international boundary, and one of the most restricted boundaries in the world. The Geneva Settlement thus failed to provide lasting peace because it created two antagonist Vietnamese nations. It failed because the Geneva powers were unwilling or unable to concert follow-up action in Vietnam to effectively supervise observance of the Accords, or to dampen the mounting tension. Mutual distrust led to incremental violations by both sides. Neither the United States nor South Vietnam was fully cooperative, but there is no evidence that either deliberately undertook to breach the peace. In contrast, the [North] proceeded to mobilize its total resources scarcely without pause from the day the peace was signed.

9

New Plan

**With Diem failing to stem the insurgency,
the U.S. increases military aid**

In the summer of 1959, it was hard to find an American official worried about Vietnam. This was not because things were going well. They were not. A National Intelligence Estimate [NIE] published in August portrayed Diem as unpopular, his economy as developing less rapidly than its rival in the North, and his government under pressure from guerrillas encouraged and, in part, supported from the North. Nevertheless, the NIE suggested no crisis then or for the foreseeable future. Diem would remain as President "for many years."

From then on, the classified record through the end of 1961 shows a succession of bleak appraisals of the regime's support in the cities and among the military, almost always accompanied by increasingly bleak estimates of increased strength and activity in the countryside [by the Viet Cong, as the Viet Minh fighting in the South was now called]. In November [1960], a military coup barely failed to overthrow Diem. The U.S. Ambassador [Elbridge Durbrow] in Saigon cabled President [Dwight] Eisenhower [soon after.]

Durbrow: The situation in Vietnam is highly dangerous to U.S. interests. Communists are engaged in large-scale guerrilla effort to take over countryside and oust Diem's government. In addition, Diem is faced with widespread popular dissatisfaction with his government's inability to stem the Communist tide and its own heavy-handed methods of operation. It seems clear that if he is to remain in power he must meet these two challenges. Should he not do so, we may well be forced, in not too distant future, to undertake difficult task of identifying and supporting alternate leadership.

In late January [1961, as President John] Kennedy took office, a Vietnam Counter-Insurgency Plan reached the White House. [In it] the U.S. offered

Diem equipment and supplies to outfit a 20,000 man increase in his army [and] to train, outfit, and supply a 32,000-man [increase] of the Civil Guard. On the [political] side, [it stressed shoring] up the regime's support within the cities by such steps as bringing opposition leaders into the government and giving the National Assembly the power to investigate charges of mismanagement and corruption. The Plan also called for "civic action" and other steps to increase the chance of winning positive loyalty from the peasants. The view that was presented to senior officials in Washington essentially showed the VC threat as a problem which could be pretty confidently handled, given a little more muscle for the army and some shaping up by the Vietnamese administration. Any doubts expressed went to the will and competence of the Diem regime, not to the strength of the VC, the role of Hanoi, or the adequacy of U.S. aid.

10

Advisors

As counterinsurgency fails, the U.S. quietly tries to introduce its own troops

In April, the VC threat in Vietnam [suddenly] looked worse than it had [three months earlier]. This led [the new Defense Secretary Robert] McNamara to call on [his deputy] to set up a task force to report on the situation. [The report] advocated U.S. support for a two-division increase in the [Republic of Vietnam Armed Forces and an increase in] U.S. manpower commitments that dwarfed the previous recommendations. This proposal [also] considered sending American troops for wider purposes, [though] no one at this time talked about using American units to directly fight the Viet Cong. [But] as the training-the-Vietnamese rationale seems essentially a device for getting Diem to accept the units, the noncombatant role for U.S. troops may have been a device for calming those members of the Administration who were reluctant to involve American units. In any event, President Kennedy approved quite limited military proposals.

[Still, in response to the deteriorating situation], the President announced that Gen. Maxwell Taylor would leave for Vietnam on a Presidential mission. Taylor arrived in Saigon on Oct 18 [and] met with Diem and [his Defense Minister] the following day. Taylor provided the Vietnamese a written summary of items. Item E was headed: Introduction of U.S. Combat troops. [It] proposed a flood relief task force, largely military in composition, to work with [the South] over an extended period. [Following the meeting], Taylor sent [an] "eyes only" [cable] for the President.

Taylor: It is noteworthy that this force is not proposed to clear the jungles and forests of Viet Cong guerrillas. That should be the primary task of the Armed Forces of Vietnam for which they should be specifically organized, trained, and stiffened with ample U.S. advisors. However, the U.S. troops may be called upon to engage in combat to protect themselves, their working parties, and the area in which they live. As a general reserve, they might be thrown into action (with U.S. agreement) against large, formed guerrilla bands which have abandoned the forests for attacks on major targets. But in general, our forces should not engage in small-scale guerrilla operations in the jungle. The risks of backing into a major Asian war by way of South Vietnam are present but are not impressive. North Vietnam is extremely vulnerable to conventional bombing, a weakness which should be exploited diplomatically in convincing Hanoi. By the foregoing line of reasoning, I have reached the conclusion that the introduction of a U.S. military Task Force without delay offers definitely more advantage than it creates risks and difficulties. In fact, I do not believe that our program to save [the South] will succeed without it.

Taylor's formal report, dated November 3, was followed by prominent news stories the next morning flatly stating that the President "remains strongly opposed to the dispatch of American combat troops to South Vietnam" and strongly implying that General Taylor had not recommended such a commitment.

On the Web
To learn more about Gen. Taylor's Vietnam visit, scan this code or go to http://www.historynet.com/general-maxwell-taylors-mission-to-vietnam.htm

11

Memos

U.S. defense officials urge massive troop involvement to keep Diem from collapse

On November 8, McNamara sent the following memorandum [to the President]:

McNamara: The basic issue framed by the Taylor Report is whether the U.S. shall: a. Commit itself to the clear objective of preventing the fall of South Vietnam to Communism, and b. Support this commitment by necessary immediate military actions and preparations for possible later actions. The Joint Chiefs and I have reached the following conclusions: The fall of South Vietnam to Communism would lead to the fairly rapid extension of Communist control in the rest of mainland Southeast Asia and in Indonesia. The chances are against, probably sharply against, preventing that fall by any measures short of the introduction of U.S. forces on a substantial scale. The introduction of a U.S. force of the magnitude of an initial 8,000 men in a flood relief context will be of great help to Diem. However, it will not convince the other side that we mean business. The other side can be convinced we mean business only if we accompany the initial force introduction by a clear commitment to the full objective stated above, accompanied by a warning through some channel to Hanoi that continued support of the Viet Cong will lead to punitive retaliation against North Vietnam. If we act in this way, the ultimate possible extent of our military commitment must be faced. I believe we can assume that the maximum U.S. forces required on the ground in Southeast Asia will not exceed six divisions, or about 205,000 men. In sum: We do not believe major units of U.S. forces should be introduced in South Vietnam unless we are willing to make an affirmative decision. We are inclined to recommend that we do commit the U.S. to the clear objective of preventing the fall of South Vietnam to Communism.

Three days later, McNamara joined [Secretary of State Dean] Rusk in a quite different recommendation, and one obviously more to the President's liking. Kennedy was very reluctant to send American ground forces to Vietnam, and quite possibly every bit as "strongly opposed" as the leaked news stories depicted him. This second memorandum gave him a joint recommendation from his Secretaries of State and Defense telling him just what he surely wanted to hear: that a decision on combat forces could be deferred.

12

Strategic Concept

**An alternative strategy emerges
to save Diem's government**

By late 1961, it had become clear in both Saigon and Washington that the yellow star of the Viet Cong was in the ascendancy. Much of [the] deterioration in South Vietnam was attributable, in U.S. eyes, to the manner in which Diem had organized his government, [splitting power between the military and local warlords]. The [South Vietnamese] Army was developing a potentially effective institutional framework under U.S. tutelage, [but Diem realized] that effectiveness could potentially be transferred against himself.

The U.S. attempts to secure organizational reforms within the Diem government had assumed psychological primacy by the time of Taylor's October mission. Several times Taylor stressed the importance of an overall plan for dealing with guerrillas. Diem tended

[to] avoid a clear response to this suggestion but finally indicated that he had a new strategic plan of his own, [possibly based on] the ideas of a new high-level advisor who had been in Saigon for several weeks.

The advisor was [Robert] Thompson, a British civil servant who had come from Malaya [where he had successfully dealt with another insurgency]. Thompson's plan was a potential rival to the American-advanced plans. The objective of Thompson's plan was to win loyalties rather than to kill insurgents. The peasants must be given the assurance of physical security so that economic and social improvements, the real object of the plan, could proceed without interruption. The means by which the villagers would be protected was the "strategic hamlet," a lightly guarded village because it was--by definition--in a relatively low risk area.

The U.S. was amenable to the [hamlet idea]. In February 1962, Taylor [presented] to President Kennedy a plan entitled "A Strategic Concept for South

Vietnam," which was an unabashed restatement of most of Thompson's major points and toward which [the] President had expressed a favorable disposition. [The] "strategic concept" avowedly flowed from three basic principles: that the problem in Vietnam presented by the VC was political rather than military in its essence; that an effective counter-insurgency plan must provide the people and villages with protection and physical security; and that counter-guerrilla forces must adopt the same tactics as those used by the guerrilla himself.

On the Web
To learn more about the Strategic Hamlet Program, scan this code or go to
http://en.wikipedia.org/wiki/ Strategic_Hamlet_Program

13

Withdrawal

The U.S. tries to draw down
its troop involvement

From mid-1962, the U.S. government went through a formal planning process, ostensibly designed to disengage the U.S. from military involvement in Vietnam. The motivation for the idea of phased withdrawal of U.S. forces was threefold: in part, the belief that developments in Vietnam itself were going well; in part, doubt over the efficacy of using U.S. forces in an internal war; [and thirdly,] events outside Vietnam were asserting a direct and immediate relevance for U.S. policy.

Looming foremost was the Berlin problem. Fraught with grave overtones of potential nuclear confrontation with the USSR, it reached crisis proportions in the spring of 1962 and flared anew in early summer. The burgeoning [Cuban missile crisis, also,] was taking on a pressing urgency. [And] finally, the

U.S., its objectives frustrated in Laos, had decided to salvage as much as possible by settling for neutralization [of that country]. It was in this context that the U.S. decided to pursue actively the policy objective of divesting itself of direct military involvement of U.S. personnel in the Vietnam insurgency.

In July 1962, at the behest of the President, [McNamara] undertook to reexamine the situation there with a view to assuring that it be brought to a successful conclusion within a reasonable time. Accordingly, he called a full-dress conference on Vietnam at CINCPAC [Commander in Chief, Pacific] Headquarters in Hawaii. The series of briefings and progress reports presented at the conference depicted a generally favorable situation. Impressed, McNamara acknowledged that the "tremendous progress" in the past six months was gratifying. He noted, however, that these achievements had been the result of short-term ad hoc actions on a crash basis. What was needed now was to conceive a long-range concerted program of systematic measures for training and equipping the [South Vietnamese forces] and for phasing out major U.S. advisory and logistic support activities. The Secretary then asked how long a period it would take before the VC could be expected to be eliminated as a significant force. [The Commander, U.S. Military Assistance, Vietnam] estimated about one year. The Secretary said that a conservative view had to be taken and to assume it would take three years instead of one, that is, by the latter part of 1965. The Joint Chiefs of Staff formally directed CINCPAC to develop a Comprehensive Plan for South Vietnam. In March, 1963, the JCS forwarded [the requested plan] to the Secretary. [In reviewing it,] McNamara was not satisfied with either the high funding levels or the adequacy regarding exactly how South Vietnam's forces were to take over from the U.S. He decided to withhold action pending full review of the [plan] at another Honolulu conference.

At the [follow-up] Conference, briefing reports again confirmed gratifying progress in the military situation. With regard to phasing out U.S. forces, however, the Secretary stated that the pace contemplated in the [plan] was too slow. He wanted it revised to accomplish a more rapid withdrawal by accelerating training programs in order to speed up replacement of U.S. units by [South Vietnamese] units as fast as possible. Specifically toward this end, he decided that 1,000 U.S. military personnel should be withdrawn from South Vietnam by the end of 1963 and directed that concrete plans be so drawn up

On the web
To learn more about the Cuban missile crisis, scan this code or go to http://en.wikipedia.org/wiki/ Cuban_missile_crisis

14

Buddhist Crisis

A religious confrontation brings
Diem to the brink

While the withdrawal planning [was] going on, significant developments were
occurring within South Vietnam. [An]
incident in [the ancient capitol city]
Hue, that precipitated what came to be
called the Buddhist crisis, happened
both inadvertently and unexpectedly.
No one then foresaw that it would gen-
erate a national opposition movement
capable of rallying virtually all non-
communist dissidence in South Vietnam.

The religious origins of the incident are
traceable to the massive flight of Catholic refugees from North Vietnam after
the French defeat in 1954. An estimated one million Catholics fled the
North and resettled in the South. Diem
accorded these Catholic refugees prefer-
ential treatment. They came to fill almost all important civilian and military

positions. As an institution, the Catholic Church enjoyed a special legal status. The Catholic primate, Ngo Dinh Thuc, was Diem's brother and advisor. Prior to 1962, there had been no outright discrimination. However, among South Vietnam's 3-4 million practicing Buddhists and the 80% of the population who were nominal Buddhists, the regime's favoritism, authoritarianism, and discrimination created a smoldering resentment.

In April 1963, the government ordered provincial officials to enforce a long-standing but generally ignored ban on the public display of religious flags. The order came just after the officially encouraged celebrations in Hue commemorating the 25th anniversary of the ordination of Diem's brother, the Archbishop, during which Papal flags had been prominently flown. The order also came just prior to Buddha's birthday [on] (May 8)--a major Buddhist festival. Not surprisingly, then, the Buddhists in Hue defiantly flew their flags in spite of the order. Seeing the demonstration as a challenge, local officials tried to disperse the crowds. When preliminary efforts produced no results, the Catholic deputy province chief ordered his troops to fire. In the ensuing melee, nine persons were killed, including some children. Armored vehicles allegedly crushed some of the victims. The Diem government subsequently put out a story that a Viet Cong agent had thrown a grenade into the crowd and that the victims had been crushed in a stampede. It steadfastly refused to admit responsibility even when neutral observers produced films showing government troops firing on the crowd.

The following day in Hue, over 10,000 people demonstrated in protest of the killings. It was the first of the long series of protest activities with which the Buddhists were to pressure the regime in the next four months. Throughout the early days of the crisis, the U.S. press had closely covered the events and brought them to the attention of the world. On June 11, the press was tipped off to be at a downtown intersection at noon. Expecting another protest demonstration, they were horrified to witness the first burning suicide by a Buddhist monk. The fiery death shocked the world and electrified South Vietnam.

After the suicide, the U.S. intensified its already considerable pressure on the government to mollify the Buddhists and to bring the deteriorating political situation under control. Finally, on June 16, a joint communiqué was released outlining the elements of a settlement. [Another one of Diem's brothers, Ngo Dinh Nhu, head of the secret police], immediately undertook to sabotage the agreement by secretly calling on the government-sponsored youth organizations to denounce it. The evident lack of faith on the part of the government in the agreement discredited the conciliatory policy of moderation that the older Buddhist leadership had followed until that time. Leadership of the Buddhist movement passed to a younger, more radical set of monks, with more far-reaching political objectives. They made intelligent and skillful political use of a rising tide of popular support.

In August, Buddhist militancy reached new intensity; monks burned themselves to death on the 5th, 15th, and 18th. The taut political atmosphere in Saigon in mid-August should have suggested to U.S. observers that a showdown was on the way. When the showdown came in the August 21 raids on the [Buddhist] pagodas, the U.S. mission was caught completely off guard. The raids were carried out after a decree placing the country under military martial law had been issued. They were conducted by combat police and special forces units taking orders directly from Nhu, not through the Army chain of command. The sweeping attacks resulted in the wounding of about 30 monks, the arrest of over 1,400 Buddhists, and the [looting and] closing of the pagodas.

On the Web
To view a video about President Kennedy and the Buddhist crisis, scan this code or go to http://www.youtube.com/watch?v=UM3uaXp8DAk&feature=related

15

Assassinations

**The murders of Diem and a U.S. President
change the direction of the war**

By the middle of September, President
[Kennedy] was deeply concerned over
the critical political situation, but more
importantly, over its effect on the war.
On September 21, the President directed [McNamara and Taylor], to proceed to Vietnam for a personal examina-
tion of the military aspects of the situation. Emerging from the investigations
and appraisals was a body of positive
evidence indicating that conditions were
good and prospects improving. In fact,
in the course of these reassurances, the
Secretary decided to order a speed up of
the planned program for release of U.S.
forces. In contrast to the generally favorable military situation, however,
there were grave misgivings about the
political state of affairs. On November
1, the political situation fell apart. The
long-anticipated coup [against Diem]
occurred. The regime was overthrown,

and both Diem and [his brother] Nhu were assassinated. A military junta of politically inexperienced generals took over the government as their successors.

On November 20, at the President's direction, a special all-agencies conference on Vietnam was convened in Honolulu for a "full-scale review." [The new] Ambassador, [Henry Cabot] Lodge, assessed the prospects for Vietnam as hopeful. In his estimation, the new government was not without promise. [He] advocated continuing to pursue the goal of setting dates for phasing out U.S. activities and turning them over to the Vietnamese. He volunteered that the announced withdrawal of 1,000 troops by the end of 1963 was already having a salutary effect.

On November 22, President Kennedy was assassinated. The consequences were to set an institutional freeze on the direction and momentum of U.S. Vietnam policy. Universally operative was a desire to avoid change of any kind during the critical interregnum period of the new Johnson Administration. The only hint that something might be different from on-going plans came in a Secretary of Defense memo for the President. In that memo, McNamara said that the new South Vietnamese government was confronted by serious financial problems, and that the U.S. must be prepared to raise planned [military assistance] levels.

16

Worse

A new U.S. President learns that South Vietnam's collapse is imminent

In [the final days of 1963,] conflicting estimates of the situation in Vietnam indicated that the bright hopes and predictions of the past were increasingly less than realistic. A McNamara memo to the President written following a trip to Vietnam of December 21 was laden with gloom.

McNamara: The situation is very disturbing. Current trends, unless reversed in the next 2-3 months, will lead to neutralization at best and more likely to a Communist-controlled state. The new government is the greatest source of concern. It is indecisive and drifting.

Unsureness about the actual state of affairs prompted the dispatching to Vietnam in early February of a CIA "Special [Investigation] Group" for an independent evaluation of the military situation.

A series of four reports were produced. Instead of finding progress, these reported a serious and steadily deteriorating situation. Cited were VC gains in the past several months, and particularly noted was that VC arms were increasing in quantity and quality. As for the Strategic Hamlet Program, they found it "at present at virtual standstill." A major conference again convened at CINCPAC headquarters for a broad reassessment. The consensus was that the military situation was definitely deteriorating. No longer was the issue whether it was progressing satisfactorily or not. The question now was how much of a setback had there been and what was needed to make up for it. The approved U.S. military strength ceiling for Vietnam was raised by more than 1500 so that total in-country authorization came to over 17,000. Further increases were in sight.

17

Happy New Year!

The U.S. tries to put the best face on another coup

There was hope that as 1964 [began] the situation [in Vietnam] would take a turn for the better. [McNamara] managed to maintain the earlier philosophy that the U.S. involvement would remain limited and that in fact the counterinsurgency effort could not really attain its goals unless the U.S. role continued to be limited and the South Vietnamese did the main job themselves.

McNamara: It is a Vietnamese war. They are going to have to assume the primary responsibility for winning it. Our policy is to limit our support to lo- gistical and training support.

Within a day or two after this testimony, there [was a coup in Saigon, the second one in three months. This] constituted not only another hard blow to our efforts in Vietnam but also to our confidence that we knew what was going on there. The first warning of [this] coup [came] January 28, when Gen. [Nguyen] Khanh told [a U.S.] advisor that pro-French, pro-neutralist members of the Military Revolutionary Committee, [the group which had deposed and murdered Diem,] were planning a palace coup that would take place [against the President, Gen. Duong Van Minh] as early as January 31. Once [their] coup was effected, they would call for neutralization of South Vietnam. [The following day,] Gen. Khanh talked to Ambassador Lodge. Khanh had apparently made an impression on the Ambassador, asking for assurance that the U.S. opposed neutralization. Lodge sensed the intent of a coup, but did not appreciate its imminence. [For] it was a matter of only about seven hours [later that Khanh decided to depose Minh himself rather than give the opportunity to others.]

The U.S. chose to view the act as merely a change of personnel within the same format. The Ambassador's first attempt to explain the affair revealed his hope that an effort to put a good face on it might not be amiss.

Lodge: Gen. Khanh's coup was obviously extremely disconcerting at first blush. We felt we were beginning to make real progress here in making Gen. Minh into a popular figure.

Privately, we continued, to be deeply chagrined and even shaken that we had not seen the coup coming. We recognized it was a severe blow to the stability of government that we had believed was so necessary for South Vietnam. We doubted the charges that Khanh used as a justification for his actions. But we accepted his explanations, promised to support him, and hoped for the best.

On the Web
To learn more about the 1964 coup, scan this code or go to http://en.wikipedia.org/wiki/1964_South_Vietnamese_coup

18

Deepening Gloom

The U.S. begins to shift its approach

Among the flood of Situation Reports that came in soon after the coup was "Commander's Personal Military Assessment." This was a report that [Gen. Paul Harkins, the first commander of Military Assistance Command, Vietnam,] had been directed to [produce] in order to establish checkpoints by which to measure progress.

Harkins: Analysis disclosed that, in spite of political turbulence, a satisfactory tempo of operation was maintained during this quarter.

[But] when [Harkins] turned to the major areas of military action, first in the north and center and later in the Delta:

Harkins: There was little substantial progress toward completing the military [objectives] in either of the two major regions.

But [Harkins] seemed to have been so thoroughly imbued with a chin-up, never-say-die spirit that he rejected the pessimistic implications which he explicitly acknowledged:

Harkins: The experiences of the last quarter disclosed the extent to which military opportunities are dependent upon political and psychological accomplishments.

No one disputed the principle that everything depended on a stable government in Saigon. Nevertheless, emphasis shifted toward greater [focus] on military operations, perhaps for the pressing reason that the VC were out now in increasing numbers, with more and better weapons, seeming to invite, if not to require, conventional military operations.

19

NSAM 288

The U.S. plans for greater involvement

[In March 1964, McNamara and Taylor visited Vietnam again] on a fact-finding mission. In the course of five days, the details of a program were decided upon in the light of views and information elicited from [U.S.] and South Vietnam officials. The program was reported orally to President [Johnson], then presented formally [as] National Security Action Memorandum 288. NSAM 288 outlined a program that called for considerable enlargement of U.S. effort. It involved an assumption by the United States of a greater part of the task, and an increased involvement by the United States in the internal affairs of South Vietnam, and for these reasons it carried with it an enlarged commitment of U.S. prestige to the success of our effort in that area.

No major reductions of U.S. personnel in the near future were expected, but it continued to be the basic policy that there would be gradual U.S. withdrawal from participation. It was conceded, however, that "the situation has unquestionably been growing worse, at least since September..." The machinery of political control extending from Saigon down to the hamlets had virtually disappeared following the November coup. Forty percent of the territory was then under the Viet Cong control. Large groups of the population displayed signs of apathy and indifference. Draft-dodging was high. Desertion rates within the Army and the [Civil Guard] were particularly high and increasing. But the Viet Cong were recruiting energetically and effectively.

On the Web
To learn more about the Viet Cong, scan this code or go to http://en.wikipedia.org/wiki/Viet_Cong

20

North

South Vietnam's new leader urges the U.S. to attack North Vietnam

Although Khanh's coup had surprised us and even shaken our confidence somewhat, we quickly made him our boy. We hoped he could somehow subdue the politically active Buddhists, the Catholic political activists, and the miscellaneous ambitious colonels and generals. But execution of the [NSAM] 288 program began to fall behind the plans. There seemed to be a business as usual attitude in the central government, and the strength of the [armed forces] declined. As we pressured Khanh to adopt reforms to remedy the deficiencies of the administration of programs within South Vietnam, his frustrations over these difficulties and failures were increased. He had no taste for the long, unspectacular social reform and social rebuilding that were the tasks of pacification. He soon began to talk increasingly of a scapegoat--a march to the

North. He wanted to get the struggle over with [and not "prolong the agony."]

[The Secretary of Defense] made a brief visit to Saigon on May 12. Khanh met with McNamara, Lodge, Taylor, and Harkins; and judging from the report of the meeting sent in by the Ambassador, Khanh put on a masterful performance. He began his talk by reviewing the recent course of the war claiming to have established control over some three million Vietnamese citizens. However, the danger of re-infiltration by the Communists still existed. Khanh said that the biggest and most time-consuming problems were political, and he was unskilled in such things and wanted to lean for advice on Ambassador Lodge. But religious problems were also pressing between Catholics and Buddhists. There was also a problem with the press. Khanh said that he was a soldier, not a politician, and wished he could spend his time mounting military operations and in planning long-term strategy instead of dealing with political intrigues and squabbles. But he had to think about the security of his regime.

[McNamara] then referred to [Lodge's] report of Khanh's desire not to "prolong the agony," and said that he wanted to hear more about this. Khanh said that in speaking of not wanting to "make the agony endure" he did not mean he would lose patience, but rather wanted to speed up the effort.

Khanh: Whereas the north attacks us with guerrillas that squirm through the jungle, we would attack them with guerrillas of our own, only ours would fly at treetop level and blow up key installations. To destroy the monster, it is necessary to strike the head.

On the Web
To learn more about Gen. Nguyen Khanh, scan this code or go to http://en.wikipedia.org/wiki/ Nguyen_Khanh

21

Phased Expansion

Top U.S. leaders plan a secret expansion of military involvement

On May 26, President [Johnson] sent out to [Ambassador] Lodge his call for [a new policy formation]:

Johnson: I have been giving the most intense consideration to the whole battle for Southeast Asia, and I have now instructed Dean Rusk, Bob McNamara, Max Taylor, and John McCone to join [Adm. Harry] Felt in Honolulu for a meeting with you, [Ambassador,] and a very small group of your most senior associates in Southeast Asia to review for my final approval a series of plans for effective action. We would like you...to be prepared to discuss with us several proposals...perhaps the most radical...is the one which...would involve a major infusion of U.S. efforts into a group of selected provinces where Vietnamese seem currently unable to execute their pacification programs. We would therefore propose that U.S. personnel, both civilian and military, drawn from the U.S. establishment currently in Vietnam, be "encadred" into current Vietnamese political and military structure...U.S. personnel assigned to these functions would not appear directly in the chain of command...They would instead be listed as "assistants" to the Vietnamese officials. In practice, however, we would expect them to carry a major share of the burden of decision and action.

On the same day that the foregoing policy guidance went out to Lodge, a meeting was held in Washington [of senior Administration officials to consider] a policy memo covering most of the same points raised in the message to [the Ambassador]. The [policy memo] proposed a phased expansion of the U.S. role. [Furthermore,] the critical question of pressures against North Vietnam [persisted.] The consensus of those formulating policy proposals for final approval by highest authority appears to have been that these pressures would have to be resorted to sooner or later.

But the subject was politically explosive, especially in a presidential election year.

[The Honolulu Conference was held May 30. Among various actions they agreed upon were to add U.S. personnel. The conference members also discussed the possibility of direct Chinese troop involvement to counter an increased U.S. presence. The military participants] responded emphatically that there was no possible way to hold off the communists on the ground without the use of tactical nuclear weapons, and that it was essential that commanders be given the freedom to use these as had been assumed in the various plans. At Honolulu, both Lodge and Westmoreland said the situation would remain in its current stalemate unless some "victory" was introduced. Westmoreland defined victory as determination to take some new military commitments such as air strikes against the Viet Cong in the Laos corridor; while Lodge defined victory as willingness to make punitive air strikes against North Vietnam. The problem before the assembled U.S. policy-makers, therefore, was to find some means of breakthrough into an irreversible commitment of the U.S.

On the Web
To view a video of President Johnson's response to the Gulf of Tonkin incident, or what became the eventual "victory," scan this code or go to http://www.youtube.com/watch?v=Dx8-ffiYyzA

22

Changing the Guard

U.S. covert operations provoke a
North Vietnamese response

The changing of the guard in the U.S. mission in Saigon at the half year point, symbolized the growing importance attached by the U.S. to its Southeast Asia commitment. The combination of [Gen. Taylor] as [the new] Ambassador, backed up by a Deputy Ambassador in the person of Alexis Johnson, made a prestigious and impressive team. They set out immediately to systematize U.S. operations. [Taylor] did not delay in plunging into the substance of the problems that were plaguing Vietnam. He asked Khanh about the status of the religious problem, and according to Taylor's report of the conversation, Khanh said the situation was still delicate. When the Ambassador queried [him] about the progress of the recruiting effort, Khanh said that it was not going as well as he would like. [And on] the question of high desertion rates, Khanh appears to have replied rather fuzzily. He said that the problem was complicated by many factors, that the Vietnamese liked to serve near home and sometimes left one service to join another. He implied that the figures might not mean exactly what they seemed to mean.

[On August 2, the "victory" that U.S. officials in Saigon had been seeking occurred.] The destroyer *USS Maddox* [was] attacked in the Tonkin Gulf by patrol craft while on patrol off the North Vietnam coast. After strenuous efforts to confirm the [aggression], President [Johnson] authorized reprisal air strikes against the North. At the time, the President briefed Congressional leaders and had a resolution of support for U.S. policy introduced. On August 7, it [was] passed with near-unanimity by both Houses of Congress. That same day, Khanh declared a state of emergency in South Vietnam which gave him near-dictatorial powers.

[Taylor resisted Khanh's control grab, and for a brief period the Military Revolutionary Council adopted a citizen-led constitution and named a prominent individual as Premier, returning the government to civilian control.]

[On November 3, 1964,] President Johnson was re-elected with a crushing majority over Barry Goldwater. He called for an in-depth review of U.S. policy and options for Vietnam. A task force led by [Assistant Secretary of State] William Bundy studied and then offered various choices for the Administration's National Security Council's Principals. The Principals submitted a two-phase recommendation to the President. The first was a slight intensification of current covert operations in the North and in Laos, the second, a moderate campaign of air strikes against the North. On December 1, the President, in a meeting with the Principals and Taylor, heard the [Ambassador's] report on the grave conditions in South Vietnam. He approved [the covert operations], and he gave tentative approval to [air strikes] but made [them] contingent on improvement by South Vietnam. On December 14, U.S. aircraft began Operation Barrel

Roll (armed reconnaissance against in-filtration routes in Laos). [But] this and other signs of increased American com-mitment against North Vietnam's in-volvement showed no results in increas-ing the South's stability, [and soon a struggle ensued to curb the power of the civilian leadership. Khanh and other officers ousted the government and nominated a military leader.]

[In the midst of the on-going political chaos, the U.S. suffered a major attack. On February 7, at Pleiku, Vietcong guerrillas carried out well-coordinated raids on a U.S. advisors' barracks and a U.S. helicopter base in the Central Highlands. This was the heaviest as-sault to date on American servicemen and installations in Vietnam. The U.S. responded with planned reprisal air at-tacks known as Flaming Dart. National Security Advisor McGeorge Bundy— brother of William Bundy—and other senior U.S. advisors were in Saigon]. On the return trip to Washington, the group drafted a memorandum for the President. The memo reported the situation in Vietnam was deteriorating and said defeat was inevitable unless the United States intervened militarily by bombing the North to persuade Hanoi to cease and desist.

In Saigon, [a newly formed group of younger military officers, known as the Armed Forces Council, resisted Gen. Khanh's efforts to regain control. They selected a new cabinet nominally headed by a civilian.] Immediately, another coup was attempted but thwarted. [The Council responded by removing Khanh from what remained of his position of authority.] Days later, February 24, [the sustained air campaign against North Vietnam] Operation Rolling Thunder began, and Khanh left for foreign parts.

On the Web
To view a report about the Viet Cong attacks on Pleiku, scan this code or go to: http://www.youtube.com/watch?feature=endscreen&v=qwp_cIL5XwY&NR=1

23

Game of Points

U.S. lays out a new plan

Early in March, the Chief of Staff of the Army evaluated the need for added supporting actions in Vietnam. His party was briefed by [Ambassador] Taylor [who observed] the basic unresolved problem as the provision of adequate security for the population. Inability to suppress the insurgency was considered largely the consequence of insufficient trained paramilitary and police manpower. Secondly, South Vietnam's open frontiers could not be sealed against infiltration. [Thirdly,] counter-insurgency was plagued by popular apathy and dwindling morale, some the consequences of a long and seemingly endless war.

On March 8, 1965, the first two Marine battalions landed at Danang. Almost all of the intelligence reports during that month indicated our programs in Vietnam were either stalemated or failing.

Not only was [South Vietnam's armed forces] strength considerably below the goals set and agreed upon, it was in considerable danger of actually decreasing. [Once again], Taylor returned to Washington for policy conferences. In the National Security Council meeting of April 1, President [Johnson] gave his formal approval, to [a] 41-point program of non-military actions submitted by Taylor. The President further approved the urgent exploration of the covert actions proposed by the Director of Central Intelligence. [And] finally, he repeated his previous approval of the 21-point program of military actions recommended by [the Army Chief of Staff]. The President [also] authorized the 18,000 to 20,000-man increase in U.S. military support forces, the deployment of two additional Marine battalions, and the change of mission for all Marine battalions to permit their use in active combat. [This approval became National Security Action Memorandum 328.]

NSAM 328 did not last long as a full and current statement of U.S. policy.

[That] policy was promptly and sharply reoriented in the direction of greater military involvement with a proportionate de-emphasis of the direct counterinsurgency efforts. On April 7, the President made his famous Johns Hopkins speech in which he publicly committed the United States more than ever before to the defense of South Vietnam, but also committed himself to engage in unconditional discussions [with North Vietnam]. The following day, [DRV Foreign Minister] Pham Van Dong published his Four Points in what seemed a defiant and unyielding response.

Pham Van Dong: [Neutralization of North and South Vietnam. Settlement of South Vietnam's internal affairs. Peaceful reunification. Withdrawal of all U.S. military forces.]

On the Web

To view President Johnson's address at Johns Hopkins University, scan this code or go to http://www.youtube.com/watch?v=vh_kHVYnUto

24

Strong Experiments

U.S. takes over the war

This sharp DRV rebuff of the President's initiative may well have accelerated the re-orientation. Within two days, messages went out from Washington indicating that decisions had been made at the highest level to go beyond the measures specified in NSAM 328. On April 15, [National Security Advisor McGeorge] Bundy sent a personal [message] to [Ambassador] Taylor saying that some explanation might be helpful.

Bundy: The President has repeatedly emphasized his personal desire for a strong experiment in the encadrement of U.S. troops with the Vietnamese. He is also very eager to see prompt experiments in use of energetic teams of U.S. officials in support of provincial governments under unified U.S. leadership. The President's belief is that current situation requires use of all practical means of strengthening position in South Vietnam and that additional U.S. troops are important, if not decisive, re-inforcements.

In addition to these steps, which were intended to increase the military effectiveness of the counter-guerrilla campaign, a series of other steps was proposed. The one that caused considerable subsequent discussion was the experimental introduction into the provincial government structure of a team of U.S. Army civil affairs personnel to assist in the establishment of stable provincial administration and to initiate and direct the political, economic, and security programs. Hot on the heels of this message came another on April 16 explaining in some further detail the proposition to experiment with U.S. civil affairs officers in the pacification program. This last message was, for Taylor, the straw that broke the camel's back. Immediately upon receiving it, the Ambassador dispatched a [message of his own] to Bundy:

Taylor: Contrary to the firm understanding which I received in Washington, I was not asked to concur in this massive visitation. For your information, I do not concur. If South Vietnam gets word of these plans to impose U.S. military government framework on their country (as this new concept seems to imply), it will have a very serious impact on our relations here. We are rocking the boat at a time when we have it almost on an even keel. I recommend that we suspend action on this project until we have time to talk over its merits and decide how to proceed with order.

A hastily arranged meeting in Honolulu on April 20 was called to soothe Taylor's temper over the hasty decisions to deploy third country troops, and to get agreement to them by the senior U.S. policy officials concerned -- not to reverse those policies or to shift the direction of our commitments. By that point we were inexorably committed to a military resolution of the insurgency. The problem seemed no longer soluble by any other means.

25

Escalate

**U.S. defense officials debate
increased involvement**

During the last days of June [1965,] with U.S. air operations against North Vietnam well into their fifth month, with U.S. forces in South Vietnam embarking for the first time upon major ground combat operations, and with the President near a decision that would increase American troop strength in Vietnam from 70,000 to over 200,000, Under-Secretary of State George Ball sent to his colleagues among the small group of Vietnam "principals" in Washington a memorandum warning that the United States was poised on the brink of a military and political disaster.

Ball: Once large numbers of U.S. troops are committed to direct combat they will begin to take heavy casualties in a war they are ill-equipped to fight in a non-cooperative if not downright hostile countryside. Once we suffer large casualties, we will have started a well-nigh irreversible process. Our involvement will be so great that we cannot--without national humiliation--stop short of achieving our complete objectives.

Ball's argument was perhaps most antithetic to one being put forward at the same time by Secretary of State Rusk.

Rusk: The integrity of the U.S. commitment is the principal pillar of peace throughout the world. If that commitment becomes unreliable, the communist world would draw conclusions that would lead to our ruin and almost certainly to a catastrophic war.

At the same time that [Ball] and Rusk wrote these papers, William Bundy also went on record with recommendations for the conduct of the war. Bundy's paper argued for a delay in further U.S. troop commitments and in escalation of the bombing campaign against North Vietnam, but a delay only in order to allow the American public time to digest the fact that the United States was engaged in a land war on the Asian mainland, and for U.S. commanders to make certain that their men were, in fact, capable of fighting effectively in conditions of counterinsurgency warfare without either arousing the hostility of the local population or causing the Vietnamese government and army simply to ease up and allow the Americans to "take over" their war.

For Defense Secretary McNamara, however, the military situation in South Vietnam was too serious to allow the luxury of delay. In a [Draft Presidential Memorandum] on July 1, he recommended an immediate decision to increase the U.S. [and] third country presence and a change in the mission of these forces from one of providing support and reinforcement for the ARVN to one which soon became known as "search and destroy." [Because there were contending outlooks for increased U.S. involvement in Vietnam,] the President wanted more information. He asked McNamara to go on another fact-gathering trip to Vietnam before submitting his final recommendations. [When McNamara returned, he now] recommended a gradual increase in the number of strike sorties against North Vietnam, [and his] memorandum concluded with an optimistic forecast.

McNamara: The overall evaluation is that the course of action recommended in this memorandum--if the military and political moves are properly integrated and executed with continuing vigor and visible determination--stands a good chance of achieving an acceptable outcome within a reasonable time in Vietnam.

Never again while he was Secretary of Defense would McNamara make so optimistic a statement about Vietnam--except in public.

On the web
To learn more about Robert McNamara, scan this code or go to
http://en.wikipedia.org/wiki/
Robert_McNamara

26

Incremental

U.S. military argues for greater force

The [bombing of North Vietnam] continued to expand and intensify, [although]
there was no sudden escalation. Interdiction remained the chief criterion for
target selection, and caution continued
to be exercised with respect to sensitive
targets. The Secretary refused to approve an overall Joint Chiefs' concept
for fighting the Vietnam War which included much heavier Rolling Thunder
strikes against key military and economic targets coordinated with a block-
ade and mining attack on North Vietnam ports.

McNamara: We've said time after time:
It is not our objective to destroy the
Government of North Vietnam. We're
not seeking to widen the war. We do
have a limited objective, and that's why
our targeting is limited as it is.

The Secretary's arguments had difficult

sledding, however. As 1965 ended, the bombing restrictions were still under attack. The U.S. was heavily engaged in the ground war in the South, and a limited bombing campaign in the North did not make much sense to those who wanted to win it. Adm. Ulysses S. Grant Sharp [Commander-in-Chief, Pacific] pleaded with McNamara to expand Rolling Thunder.

Sharp: The aim should be to drastically reduce the flow of military supplies reaching the North Vietnam and hence the VC. The armed forces of the United States should not be required to fight this war with one arm tied behind their backs.

[On] January 24, [1966, another] memorandum from McNamara for the President recommended an increase in the number of attack sorties against North Vietnam. Most of [his] memorandum dealt with the planned expansion of American ground forces, however. Such an increase in U.S. combat strength would raise total U.S. personnel in Vietnam from 220,000 to over

400,000. [When] this slightly enlarged campaign opened, the Chiefs filed a memorandum [of their own] stressing the special importance of an early attack on North Vietnamese POL [petroleum, oil, lubricants]. The President only approved giving commanders discretion to launch sorties on the fringe of the prohibited circles around Hanoi and Haiphong. He did not consent to measures involving more visible escalation of the air war. This possibility could widen the war if it were taken by North Vietnam and its allies as indicating a U.S. decision to commence "all-out" bombing aimed at an "unlimited" objective.

On the web

To learn more about the bombing campaign Operation Rolling Thunder, scan this code or go to http:// en.wikipedia.org/wiki/ Operation_Rolling_Thunder

27

POL Attacks

U.S. military continues to push for greater force, while civilian leaders question results

The spring of 1966 saw one of the most determined and most public efforts by the international community to bring the U.S. and North Vietnam to the negotiating table. While at no time during this peace initiative was there any evidence of give in either side's uncompromising position, the widespread publicity of the effort meant that the Administration was constrained from any military actions that might be construed as "worsening the atmosphere." While [the Administration] was fending off this international pressure for an end to the bombing and de-escalation of the war as a means to peace, the President was having increasing trouble with war-dissenters within his own party. [In addition, U.S.] public reaction to the simmering political crisis in South Vietnam was reflected in declining popular approval of the President's performance.

In March, 68% of those polled had approved the President's conduct in office, but by May, his support had declined sharply to only 54%. Sometime in late May, the President decided that attacks on the entire North Vietnamese POL network could not be delayed much longer.

The strikes were launched on June 29. The large Hanoi tank farm was apparently completely knocked out; the Haiphong facility looked about 80 percent destroyed. The Deputy Commander of the 7th Air Force in Saigon called the operation "the most significant, the most important strike of the War." Strikes continued on the other major POL storage sites and were soon accepted as a routine part of the bombing program.

While [Adm. Sharp] and his subordinates were making every effort to hamstring North Vietnam logistical operation through the POL attacks, [McNamara] was keeping tabs on results through specially commissioned reports from [Institute for Defense

Analyses].   What became clearer and
clearer as the summer wore on was that
while we had destroyed a major portion
of North Vietnam's [petroleum] storage
capacity, she retained enough dispersed
capacity to meet her on-going requirements.   The greater invulnerability of
dispersed POL meant an ever mounting
U.S. cost in munitions, fuel, aircraft
losses, and men.   By August, we were
reaching the point at which these costs
were prohibitive.   It was simply imprac-
tical and infeasible to attempt any further constriction of North Vietnam's
POL storage capacity.   Powerful reinforcement about the ineffectiveness of
the strikes came at the end of August
when a special summer study group of
top American scientists submitted a series of reports.   One of their papers
dealt in considerable detail with the entire bombing program, generally con-
cluding that bombing had failed in all
its specified goals.   McNamara made no
effort to conceal his dissatisfaction and
disappointment.

McNamara: I don't believe that the
bombing up to the present has signifi-

cantly reduced, nor any bombing that I could contemplate in the future would significantly reduce, actual flow of men and materiel to the South.

McNamara left Washington on October 10 and spent four days in Vietnam. His findings in those days must have confirmed his disquiet about the lack of progress of the war to date, for when he returned to Washington he sent the President a gloomy report with recommendations for leveling off the U.S. effort and seeking a solution through diplomatic channels. With the war seemingly stalemated, this appeared to be the only "out" to the Secretary that offered some prospect of bringing the conflict to an end in any near future. The Chiefs opposed any curtailment of the bombing as a means to get negotiations started.

JCS: The Joint Chiefs of Staff believe our air campaign against North Vietnam to be an integral and indispensable part of our over all war effort. To be effective, the air campaign should be conducted with only those minimum constraints necessary to avoid indiscriminate killing of population.

28

More

U.S. resorts to further escalation

U.S. resorts to further escalation

The President apparently did not react immediately to the McNamara recommendations [or the Joint Chiefs' dissent]. He was at the time preparing for the Manila Conference to take place October 23. At Manila, the President worked hard to get the South Vietnamese to make a greater commitment to the war and pressed them for specific reforms. He also worked hard to get a generalized formulation of allied objectives in the war. Its most important feature was an appeal to the North Vietnamese for peace based on a commitment to withdraw forces within six months after the end of the war. Once home, [President Johnson again] deferred any major decisions on the war until after the [1966 Congressional] elections. Several "peace" candidates were aggressively challenging Administration supporters, and the President wished to do nothing that might boost their chances.

In January 1967, another effort to communicate positions with North Vietnam had been made, and there was an understandable desire to defer escalatory decisions until it had been determined whether some possibility for negotiations existed. Moreover, the Tet holiday, for which a truce had been announced, made late January an unpropitious time to expand the bombing. [U.S. Army commander] Gen. William Westmoreland had strongly recommended against a truce for Tet because of the losses to friendly forces during the Christmas and New Year's truces just concluded. The factor which eventually forced the President's hand was the unprecedented North Vietnamese resupply activity during the [Tet] bombing suspension. By the time the truce had been in effect 24 hours, surveillance revealed the massive North Vietnamese effort to move supplies south. The President perceived the strikes as necessary in the psychological test of wills between the two sides to punish the North, in spite of the near-consensus opinion of his advisers that no level of damage or destruction that we were willing to inflict was likely to destroy Hanoi's determination to continue the struggle.

On the Web
To learn more about North Vietnam's resupply efforts, scan this code or go to http://en.wikipedia.org/wiki/Viet_Cong_and_Vietnam_People's_Army_logistics_and_equipment

29

Middle Course

U.S. defense officials contend over policy

By May 1967, the opinions of McNamara and his key aides with respect to the bombing and Westmoreland's [requests for increased troops] had crystallized sufficiently that another Draft Presidential Memorandum was written. It was entitled, "Future Actions in Vietnam," and was a comprehensive treatment of all aspects of the war--military, political, and diplomatic. When added to the continuing difficulties in bringing the war in the South under control, the unchecked erosion of U.S. public support for the war, and the smoldering international disquiet about the need and purpose of such U.S. intervention, it is not hard to understand the DPM's statement that, "This memorandum is written at a time when there appears to be no attractive course of action." Nevertheless, 'alternatives' was precisely what the DPM had been written to suggest. These were introduced with a recapitulation of where we stood militarily and what the Chiefs were recommending. This articulation of American purposes and commitments in Vietnam pointedly rejected the high blown formulations of U.S. objectives in NSAM 288 and came forcefully to grips with the old dilemma of the U.S. involvement dating from the Kennedy era: only limited means to achieve excessive ends.

McNamara showed the draft to the President the same day it was completed, but there is no record of his reaction. It is worth noting, however, that May 19 was the day that U.S. planes struck the Hanoi power plant just one mile north of the center of Hanoi. That the President did not promptly endorse the McNamara recommendations, as he had on occasions in the past, is not surprising. The Chiefs were in ardent opposition to anything other than a significant escalation of the war with a call -up of reserves, in direct opposition to McNamara and his aides and created a genuine policy dilemma. The President's decision was to push onward with the bombing program essentially as it had been, continuing the bit-by-bit expansion of armed reconnaissance and striking a few new fixed targets in each Rolling Thunder series, but still holding back from closing the ports and such sensitive targets as the MiG airfields. For the moment, at least, neither the hawks nor the doves had won their case. The President had decided to postpone the issue, insuring that the partisans would continue their fight.

On the Web

To view the effects of the bombing campaign, scan this code or go to http://www.youtube.com/watch?v=4KIvAXPEcaE

30

End Run

U.S. military outmaneuvers
civilian defense leaders

In late July, Secretary was informed by
Senator [John] Stennis that the Prepar-
edness Subcommittee of the Senate
Armed Services Committee intended to
conduct extensive hearings in August
into the conduct of the air war against
North Vietnam. In addition to their intention to call the Secretary, they also
indicated that they would hear from all
the top military leaders involved in the
Rolling Thunder program including Ad-
miral Sharp. The subcommittee had
unquestionably set out to defeat McNamara. They were defenders of "air
power" and had often aligned themselves with the "professional military ex-
perts" against what they considered
"unskilled civilian amateurs." They
viewed the restraints on bombing as ir-
rational, the shackling of a major in-
strument which could help win victory.
With Vietnam blown up into a major

war, with more than half a million U.S. troops and a cost of more than $2 billion a month, and with no clear end in sight, their patience with a restrained bombing program was beginning to wear thin.

The hearings exposed to public view the serious divergence between McNamara and the country's professional military leaders. The Secretary spent [his] day on the witness stand, answering questions, rebutting charges, and debating the issues. His use of facts and figures and reasoned arguments was one of his masterful performances, but in the end he was not persuasive. The subcommittee issued a report on August 31 which castigated the Administration's conduct of the bombing campaign, deferred to the authority of the professional military judgments it had heard, accepted virtually all the military criticisms of the program, and advocated a switch-over to escalating "pressure" concepts.

31

Justified and Necessary

All restraints are removed

The Stennis report raised a furor by ex-
posing the policy rift within the Administration. In an attempt to dampen its
effect, the President called an unsched-
uled news conference on September 1 to
deny differences among his advisors
and to generally overrule his Secretary
of Defense on the bombing. More sting-
ing for McNamara, however, than this
oral repudiation must have been the
subsequent escalatory decisions against
his advice. With Hanoi complaining
that the raids [were] escalating not de-
escalating the war, the President decided to make a dramatic public attempt to overcome the communications
barrier between the two capitals. In
San Antonio, Texas, on September 29,
the President delivered a long impas-
sioned plea for reason in Hanoi.

Johnson: "Why not negotiate now?" so
many ask me. The answer is that we

and our South Vietnamese allies are wholly prepared to negotiate tonight. I am ready to talk with Ho Chi Minh tomorrow. I am ready to have Secretary Rusk meet with their Foreign Minister tomorrow. I am ready to send a trusted representative of America to any spot on this earth to talk in public or private with a spokesman of Hanoi.

After the speech, the contacts in Paris continued to [pursue] a positive response from Hanoi, but none was apparently forthcoming. With the failure of [this] peace initiative, escalatory pressures could no longer be resisted. The Chiefs sent the President a major memo outlining their understanding of the objectives of the war, the constraints within which the national authorities wished it to be fought, the artificial limitations that were impeding the achievement of our objectives, and a recommended list of ten new measures against North Vietnam. In addition, the Chiefs requested that the comprehensive prohibition of attacks in the Hanoi/ Haiphong areas be removed with the expected increase in civilian casualties to be accepted as militarily justified and necessary.

The President acceded to the wishes of the military and the political pressures from Congress. The fact that [he relented] on this vital issue at this point, when all the evidence available to McNamara suggested the continuing ineffectiveness of the bombing, must have been an important if not determining factor in the Secretary's decision in November to retire. [By the fall of 1967,] except for the port of Haiphong and a few others, virtually all of the economic and military targets in North Vietnam that could be considered even remotely significant had been hit.

32

Decibel Level Rises

The war comes home

The purely military problems of the war aside, the President was also experiencing great difficulty in maintaining public support for this conduct of the war. On October 12, the very day that Rusk was castigating the North Vietnamese in his press conference for their stubbornness, thirty dovish Congressmen sent the President an open letter complaining about the inconsistency of the recent bombing targets. A more serious problem was the massive anti-war demonstration organized in Washington on October 21. The leaders of the "New Left" assembled some 50,000 anti-war protesters in the Capitol on this October Saturday and staged a massive march on the Pentagon. And as if to add insult to injury, an impudent and dovish Senator [Eugene] McCarthy announced in November that he would be a candidate for the Democratic nomination for President. He stated his intention of running in all the primaries and of taking the Vietnam War to the American people in a direct challenge to an incumbent President and the leader of his own party. To counter these assaults on his war policy from the left, the President dramatically called home the Ambassador and Westmoreland in November and sent them out to publicly defend the conduct of the war and the progress that had been achieved.

[Concurrent with this publicity campaign,] the Institute for Defense Analyses had called together many of the people who had participated in the 1966 Summer Study for another look at the effectiveness of the bombing and at various alternatives that might get better results. Their report was submitted in mid-December 1967 and was probably the most categorical rejection of bombing as a tool of our policy in Southeast Asia to be made before or since by an official or semi-official group. The study was done for McNamara and closely held after completion. It was completed after his decision to leave the Pentagon, but it was a powerful confirmation of the positions on the bombing that he had taken in the internal councils of the government over the preceding year.

The negative analyses of the air war, however, did not reflect the official view of the Administration, and certainly not the view of the military at any level in the command structure at year's end. Contributing to the firmness of the U.S. position were the optimistic reports from the field on military progress in the war. Improvement was noted throughout the last quarter of the year and a mood of cautious hope pervaded the dispatches.

As planned, the Allies began a 36-hour truce in honor of the Tet holidays on January 29. The order was shortly canceled, however, because of fierce enemy attacks in the northern provinces. Then, suddenly on January 31, the Viet Cong and North Vietnamese Army forces launched massive assaults on virtually every major city and provincial capital, and most of the military installations in South Vietnam. In Saigon, attackers penetrated the new American Embassy and the Palace grounds before they were driven back. Whole sections of the city were under Viet Cong control temporarily. In Hue, an attacking force captured virtually the entire city. Everywhere the fighting was intense and the casualties, civilian as well as military, were staggering. Coming on the heels of optimistic reports from the field commands, this offensive stunned both the Administration and the American public.

On the Web
To a view a report on the Tet Offensive, scan this code or go to http://www.youtube.com/watch?v=q1vJqTN-qVI

Corner is Turned

Support for the U.S. President and the war comes to an end

The [Tet] crisis engendered the most soul-searching debate within the Administration about what course to take next in the whole history of the war. In the emotion laden atmosphere of those dark days, there were cries for large-scale escalation on the one side and for significant retrenchment on the other. In the end, an equally difficult decision was made--to stabilize the effort in the South and de-escalate in the North.

One of the inescapable conclusions of the Tet experience was that as an interdiction measure against the infiltration of men and supplies, the bombing had been a near total failure. Moreover, it had not succeeded in breaking Hanoi's will to continue the fight. The only other major justification for continuing the bombing was its punitive value, and that began to pale in comparison with the potential for producing negotiations with North Vietnam.

The primary focus of the U.S. reaction to the Tet offensive was another reexamination of force requirements for avoiding defeat or disaster in the South. The President sent Gen. Wheeler, the Chairman of the Joint Chiefs, to Saigon on February 23 to consult with Gen. Westmoreland and report back on the new situation and its implication for further forces.

[When] Wheeler returned from Vietnam, the substance of his and General Westmoreland's recommendations greatly troubled the President. The military were requesting a major reinforcement of more than three divisions and supporting forces totaling in excess of 200,000 men, and were asking for a call -up of some 280,000 reservists. The President was understandably reluctant to take such action, the more so in an election year.

The President asked his incoming Secretary of Defense, Clark Clifford, to convene a senior group of advisors from State, Defense, CIA, and the White House and to conduct a complete review of our involvement. The first meeting of the Clifford Group was convened in the Secretary's office at the Pentagon on Wednesday, February 28. The focus of the entire effort was the deployment requests. [Soon after,] the New York Times broke the story of Gen. Westmoreland's 200,000 man troop request in banner headlines. The following day, March 11, Secretary Rusk went before [Senator William] Fulbright's Foreign Relations Committee for the first time in two years for nationally televised hearings on U.S. war policy. In sessions that lasted late that Monday and continued on Tuesday, the Secretary was subjected to sharp questioning by virtually every member. These trying two days of testimony by Secretary Rusk was completed only hours before the results from the New Hampshire primary began to come in.

To the shock and consternation of official Washington, the President had defeated his upstart challenger, Eugene

McCarthy, who had based his campaign on a halt in the bombing and an end to the war, by only the slenderest of margins. The reaction across the country was electric. It was clear that Lyndon Johnson, the master politician, had been successfully challenged, not by an attractive and appealing alternative vote -getter, but by a candidate who had been able to mobilize and focus all the discontent and disillusionment about the war. National politics in the election year 1968 would not be the same thereafter.

Critics of the President's policies in Vietnam in both parties were buoyed by the New Hampshire results. But for Senator Robert Kennedy they posed a particularly acute dilemma. With the President's vulnerability on Vietnam now demonstrated, should Kennedy, his premier political opponent on this and other issues, now throw his hat in the ring? After four days of huddling with his advisers, and first informing both the President and Senator McCarthy, Kennedy announced his candidacy on March 16. For President Johnson, the threat was now real. McCarthy, even in the flush of a New Hampshire victory, could not reasonably expect to unseat the incumbent President. But Kennedy was another matter. The President now faced the prospect of a long and divisive battle for renomination within his own party against a very strong contender, with the albatross of an unpopular war hanging around his neck.

Johnson: Fifty-two months and 10 days ago, in a moment of tragedy and trauma, the duties of this office fell upon me. I asked then for your help and God's, that we might continue America on its course, binding up our wounds, healing our history, moving forward in new unity, to clear the American agenda and to keep the American commitment for all of our people. United we have kept that commitment. United we have enlarged that commitment. Through all time to come, I think America will be a stronger nation, a more just society, and a land of greater opportunity and fulfillment because of what we have all done together in these years of unparalleled achievement. Our reward will come in the life of freedom, peace, and hope that our children will enjoy through ages ahead. What we won when all of our people united just must not now be lost in suspicion, distrust, selfishness, and politics among any of our people. Believing this as I do, I have concluded that I should not permit the Presidency to become involved in the partisan divisions that are developing in this political year. With America's sons in the fields far away, with America's future under challenge right here at home, with our hopes and the world's hopes for peace in the balance every day, I do not believe that I should devote an hour or a day of my time to any personal partisan causes or to any duties other than the awesome duties of this office--the Presidency of your country. Accordingly, I shall not seek, and I will not accept, the nomination of my party for another term as your President. But let men everywhere know, however, that a strong, a confident, and a vigilant America stands ready tonight to seek an honorable peace--and stands ready tonight to defend an honored cause--whatever the price, whatever the burden, whatever the sacrifice that duty may require. Thank you for listening. Good night, and God bless all of you.

On the Web
To view President Johnson's address, scan this code or go to http://www.youtube.com/watch?v=2-FibDxpkb0

Resources

Videos

On the Web
To view a 1965 government video showing Robert McNamara briefing the media, scan this code or go http://www.youtube.com/watch?v=Hw0F0YF6h7o

On the Web
To view a 1965 government video rationalizing the war in Vietnam, scan this code or go to http://www.youtube.com/watch?v=qEljbPwFQ9M&feature=relmfu

On the Web
To view a 2008 long-form video on casualties of the war, go https://www.youtube.com/watch?v=4KIvAXPEcaE

On the Web
To view Episode One of Battlefield: Vietnam, a 12-part series, go to https://www.youtube.com/watch?v=n62-16kBzA&list=PL3H6zO37pboH6zS98cjo_xznKzNKEMJJj

120

Service Organizations

On the Web

To learn more about Vietnam Veterans of America, scan this code or go to http://www.vva.org/

On the Web

To learn more about services for all veterans, scan this code or go to http://maketheconnection.net/

On the Web

To learn more about Agent Orange relief, scan this code or go to http://www.vn-agentorange.org/

On the Web

To learn more about unexploded ordinance removal in Vietnam, scan this code or go to http://www.peacetreesvietnam.org/

Twelve Things

Here are items that the editor of this publication learned from reading the Pentagon Papers.

1)   During colonialism, the French divided Vietnam into three distinct areas: Tonkin (north); Annam (central); and Cochinchina (south).

2)   The French government betrayed the Vietnamese in 1946 by not fulfilling their agreement to allow Tonkin to become a free, independent state, albeit within the French union.

3)   The United States became directly involved in the war in Vietnam in 1949.

4)   The United States funded about 80% of the French war expense.

5)   The United States held that Vietnam must be preserved for the free world against Communism otherwise there would be a "domino effect" furthering the loss of other Asian nations. This theory was quietly abandoned by

the U.S. after the Geneva conference.

6)　The Geneva conference of 1954 created not two separate countries (North Vietnam and South Vietnam), but rather two "zones" that were to be united through elections in 1956. The French, and other international powers, betrayed the Vietnamese by not ensuring that these elections occur.

7)　Nearly one million Vietnamese relocated to the southern zone of Vietnam following the Geneva conference, many of them Catholics who comprised an elite class in a largely Buddhist country.

8)　There were powerful sects in South Vietnam with religious-political-military allegiances that over-rode national identity.

9)　The United States considered sending combat troops to shore up the Saigon government as early as 1961.

10) There were many high-level U.S. officials arguing against direct American involvement in Vietnam in 1965. Their

warnings were out-weighed by the arguments of competing officials.

11) The U.S. bombing strategy over North Vietnam grew to be conducted almost without limits, and yet it was determined to be costly and ineffective.

12) The person who is President makes a monumental difference. If Franklin Roosevelt had lived longer, it is likely he would have resisted France's desire to reestablish its colonial power over Indochina. His successor Harry Truman had no such qualms with French aims. Also, while John Kennedy was agreeable to advisors, military assistance, and covert operations, he was unlikely to ever send combat troops or carry out aerial bombing over North Vietnam, unlike Lyndon Johnson.

Final Word

A single observation the editor would make about the Vietnam War, inclusive of both the First Indochina War (1946-1954) and the Second Indochina War (1955-1975), is that it did not have to happen. It was a war of choice, not of necessity. All the lives that were lost, the bodies and minds that were damaged, and the hearts that were crushed were needless. It did not have to start, and it could have been stopped many times along the way. But the people who had the ability to make that decision chose instead to keep it going.

What can an ordinary person do to prevent such folly and disaster? This is a question each of us must keep asking of ourselves.

Index

domino theory, 21
Geneva, 25
infiltration, 79
invasion, 16
U.S. objectives, 49
Viet Cong, 74

Lodge, Henry Cabot
Johnson, 72
Khanh, 63-64, 70-71
new ambassador, 58
policy guidance, 73-74

McCarthy, Eugene,
candidacy 108,
campaign 115
victory 117

McNamara, Robert,
1961 memos, 42-44
1962 policy, 49
1963 JCS plan, 50
1965 memo to increase
1966 memo, 92
1966 recommendations, 97
1966 Vietnam tour, 96
1967 bombing study, 109
Adm. Sharp, 92
assassinations, 59
bombing, 94-95, 100
decision to retire, 107
draft memo 1967, 101
Honolulu, 72
hope in 1964, 62
JCS concept, 90
Khanh, 70-71
memo late-1963, 60
repudiation, 105
Senate hearing, 102-104
Study, 3
Task Force, 38
to Vietnam 1963, 57
to Vietnam 1964, 67
U.S. presence, 87-89

National Security Council
U.S. policy, 13-14

Pentagon Papers
Vietnam Study, 3-6

Roosevelt, Franklin D.
independence, 8-9

Saigon
advisor in, 46
Armed Forces Council, 80
atmosphere, 56
Cholon, 28
coup d'etat, 10
coup in, 62
Diem, 30-31
Durbrow, 36
French forces, 9
government in, 66
McNamara, 70
mission in, 76-77
negotiations, 113-114
pledge to, 6
political control, 68
Taylor, 39
U.S. advisors, 79
U.S. Air Force, 95
Viet Cong, 45

State Department
Congress, 20
records, 33

Stennis, John
report, 106
Senate Committee, 104

Taylor, Maxwell
1961 mission, 39-41
1961 report, 42

Glossary

ARVN	Army of Republic of South Vietnam
CG	Civil Guard
CIA	Central Intelligence Agency
CINCPAC	Commander in Chief, Pacific
CIP	Counterinsurgency Plan
CPSVN	Comprehensive Plan for South Vietnam
DCM	Deputy Chief of Mission
DESOTO	Destroyer patrols off North Vietnam
DMZ	Demilitarized Zone
DPM	Draft Presidential Memorandum
GVN	Government of Vietnam
IDA	Institute for Defense Analyses
JCS	Joint Chiefs of Staff
MACV	Military Assistance Command, Vietnam
MiG	Mikoyan and Gurevich (Russian aircraft)
MRC	Military Revolutionary Council
NIE	National Intelligence Estimate
NSA	National Security Agency
NSAM	National Security Action Memorandum
NVA	North Vietnam Army
NVN	North Vietnam
POL	Petroleum, oil, lubricants
PAVN	People's Army of Vietnam
RVNF	Republic of Vietnam Forces
USSR	Union of Soviet Socialist Republics
VC	Viet Cong
VM	Viet Minh